How to Be a
Good Boyfriend!

15 Easy Ways to Win Her Heart
& Keep Both of You Happy!

By
Kimberly Peters

Other Books by Kimberly Peters

Relationship Kick Starter
How to Be a Great Kisser
How to be a Good Employee
How to Be a Good Manager

Contents

Introduction   5

Basics   9

The 100% Solution   14

Treat Her Right   19

Be Understanding   30

Trust Her   37

Communicate Well   43

Compromise   52

Be Supportive   58

Notice Things About Her   67

Make Her Better   71

Make Her Feel Better About Herself   78

Be Affectionate & Loving   83

Traits for the Perfect Boyfriend   89

Sex   98

Be Spontaneous   106

Be Independent   112

Better Yourself   120

Conclusion   128

"Treat Her Like a Queen
And She Will Treat You
Like Her King!"

Introduction

When it comes to relationships, we are always looking for other people who make us happier, better and more comfortable people. We look for people who fulfill our needs and complete our lives. We look for people who just make our lives better. Those people do not need to be perfect and they do not need to look like a supermodel either.

But those people need to treat us a particular way. They need to make us feel special, needed and wanted. We also want to feel safe, secure and nurtured as well. Even thought this sounds like a huge bill to fill, the fact is most of us are capable of doing these things and much more in our relationships.

Most of the time when relationships falter or end it is because at least one person was not getting these particular needs met in the relationship. It makes no difference whether this was intentional or not. If needs are not being met then we are much more likely to look for someone else who can meet those needs.

The good news is that it is easy to meet the emotional needs within a relationship. Usually it just requires patience, a little effort and most of all, awareness. Awareness just means being aware of what you do and what your partner is looking for. If you can become aware of what is important to your partner, you will have a much better chance of success and becoming part of a long term successful relationship.

In this book we are going to cover a lot of things that people look for in partners and spouses.
While you do not have to become a master at all of these things, the more you can make part of your life the happier your partner will become with you and the relationship. So read through the book and see what things you might want to add to your personality and the way you treat and interact with your partners. Some might apply while others might not. Consider each one and try and see how you can use it to strengthen your relationship and improve its quality.

While every relationship has its ups and downs, it is important to remember one very important thing. That is the more a relationship meets or exceeds the needs of BOTH people; the less likely people are going to look outside the relationship for something more. That means if both people are getting what they need from a relationship, they will not seek out other partners or look outside the relationship for the comfort and security they need.

As you read through this book you may see things repeated throughout the book. This was done for two reasons. First and foremost, it has been our experience that most people who purchase self improvement or relationship books do so because they have a very real and important particular need.

Because they have this critical need, they often skip to the section of the book that deals with that problem. While there is nothing wrong with this approach, sometimes important information covered earlier is not available to the reader. So they might not get the full understanding of the materials.

To combat this problem, we have written and designed this book so that every chapter is a standalone short book. Everything you need to understand the topic of that chapter is provided in those pages

So if a topic pertains to more than one chapter, you might see it repeated. It is not a mistake; it is to help make sure everyone understands what they are reading.

Second, some concepts or material might be extremely important. In those cases, repetition is considered one of the best ways to learn and repeating critical information helps everyone remember it in more detail and retain it for a longer period of time.

The best way to read this book is from start to finish. But if you have an urgent need, feel free to go right to that part of the book. Then, after you have read those parts, go back to the beginning and read the book through to the end. This will give you the full picture while also addressing that urgent need as quickly as possible.

Another way to get more out of this book is to stop after every chapter and see how you can make that topic or concept relevant to your own life. Ask yourself how to apply what you just read and think about how using it will help you make your life and relationships better. When our brains see the benefit in doing something, you will give a much better effort to the process and what is required.

So let's get started discovering what you can do to become the absolute best boyfriend ever!

Basics

Let's get started on some basic things that guys need to do in order to be considered great boyfriends. These are not difficult things to do and most of you are probably doing most, if not all, of them already. If you are, that's great. If you are not, it just might be time to consider changing the way you relate to the women and other people in your life.

Here are some very basic attitudes, views and approaches you might seriously consider making towards your current or prospective girlfriend:

Understand that Everyone Has Flaws

Even if you might think you are the exception, you are not. Everyone has flaws.

No one is perfect and no one should be perfect or try to be either. Expecting someone to be without fault is to set expectations so high that it will be impossible for anyone to possibly live up to them.

Someone might be carrying a few extra pounds or not have perfect hair, pearly white teeth or be the extremely intelligent person of your dreams. That doesn't mean this person is without merit and not worthy of your attention and respect.

Take the other person for whom and what they are. Accept them with their faults and everything else they bring to the table. Appreciate them for who and what they are and do not obsess over what they might be lacking. Keep in mind that they are accepting you with all your faults as well. (Even if you think you are perfect!)

Don't Enter a Relationship with the Idea of Changing Someone

Everyone is different and we should never try to change anyone into someone they are not meant to be.

Instead, we need to be comfortable with each other and accept each other for who and what we are. If the person who needs to change is willing and enthusiastic about it, that is fine. But we should never force change upon anyone against their will.

Don't Compare Her to Others

No one likes to be compared to another person even if that comparison might be a very favorable one. Everyone is different and comparing one person to another is almost impossible to do fairly and impartially. Sometimes this can be very difficult for her, especially when it comes to physical appearance.

This is especially true when it comes to past girlfriends or other people you have dated in the past. Competing with a memory, that probably has been distorted and "cleaned up" over time can be almost impossible. If your girlfriend even thinks you are comparing her to others it might make her feel insecure and sometimes even angry. Accept people for who they are and do not compare or measure them against anyone else for any reason.

If you must compare someone to someone else, for example when you are dating more than one girlfriend and want to decide which one is best for you, make this comparison in your mind and keep it to yourself. Do not share your evaluation or the results with either person. Just make up your mind and go on with your life.

Dignity & Respect

Everyone, whether it be a girlfriend, boyfriend or the person sitting next to you on the bus deserves to be treated with dignity and respect. This is true even if that person does not treat you in the same manner. Be the person known for treating everyone very well and be the person known for caring and respecting others.

In addition to being the right way to go through life, treating people in your life very well is an endearing quality in the eyes of most females. They appreciate someone who treats them right, respects them for who they are, and just treats them with dignity and respect every single day of the week.

The Golden Rule

Most of us are aware of the golden rule and when it comes to being a great boyfriend this rule really applies. For those who are not aware of the Golden Rule, it is "Treat others like you would like to be treated." If you do this, you will very rarely be wrong.

Think about that for a minute as far as a being a boyfriend is concerned. Think about how you would like to be treated on a date, at a party, at a family gathering and even in the bedroom. Think about what you would like and dislike in those different situations.

If you are honest with yourself, you will discover that if you provide those very same things to your partner, she will likely be very happy with that as well.

Never, Ever Raise a Hand

This one should be on the list of things that should never even need to be discussed but we need to make sure everyone understands this important concept. It is NEVER all right or OK to hit or strike a woman or anyone for that matter. I don't care what the other person does to you. If they strike you or get physical, then walk away. Unless your personal safety and well being is at stake and there is absolutely 100% no other way out of the situation, you NEVER raise your hand to a woman.

If someone hits you, just leave. If someone gets physical, just leave. If you get really angry or frustrated, just leave. It is better to leave and either stay away or come back when you are calmer than stay in a situation and hit another human being.

The 100% Solution

Relationships of all kinds require efforts from all people involved in order to make them work. If just one person works to make the relationship better it is more than likely that the relationship will not survive. In order for relationships to grow and mature, both people need to make a commitment to work together to make things work. Because of this, most people believe that the responsibilities in relationships are split 50-50.

And most people would be wrong.

In order for relationships to really work, both people must give 100% not 50%. That means each person needs to assume 100% of the responsibility when it comes to making things work. It does not mean that one person has the responsibility for this and the other person has the responsibility for that.

BOTH people must assume responsibility for making EVERYTHING work in the relationship.

That does not mean that someone has to take responsibility for the actions of the other person. If one does something wrong then that person needs to take the responsibility for what they have said or done. But even in those circumstances both people have responsibility to work things out with each other.

For example, if one person shows up late for a date repeatedly, they must accept the responsibility for that. But the other person has the responsibility for accepting the apology and working through the situation so there are no lingering hard feelings or resentment. That means one person apologizes for what they did and the other person accepts the apology and both people move on.

Relationships are a partnership where both partners play a role in every part of the relationship. Both partners are equally responsible for building and repairing the relationship. If one person tries but the other refuses, the relationship will not move forward. If one person refuses to compromise and help resolve differences between both partners the relationship will suffer as well.

Another way of looking at this would be to adopt the attitude where you always ask yourself what you could do to make the situation and relationship better. That is the question you should be asking yourself. You should not ask who is responsible for the situation or the problem but rather what you might be able to do to make things better. In other words, you are accepting responsibility not for what caused this situation or the problem but for what is going to happen next.

For example, if you cause a problem or hurt your partner, your thoughts should be directed towards what you can do to make your partner feel better. That might include an apology, asking for forgiveness, explaining things to your partner or some other action or gesture. The entire florist industry is based on this type of response!

If something was done to you by your partner, you might ask yourself what your response should be moving forward. If your partner does something wrong and apologizes to you, you should graciously accept the apology when it is offered if that is what you believe should be done. That is certainly a lot better and more positive than refusing the apology and storming out the door.

That is why we say that each person should have 100% of their efforts focused on nurturing and growing the relationship.

If both people are focused in that manner many of the little problems and situations will disappear. It is amazing how differently we will act and think when we alter the focus on our thoughts.

This does not mean, however, that either party should put up with constant abuse or problems. There will always be deal breakers and treatment that will require an exit from the relationship. But those situations should be rare for most of us. If we approach the little day to day things with the 100% solution, those little things will either go away or will be resolved quickly and easily.

Another benefit of the 100% attitude is that your partner will feel more positively towards you and appreciate the way you treat them in the relationship. They will know that you "have their back" and no matter what the situation, you will be there to help and support them. They will also realize that they can make a mistake and that they don't have to be perfect. IN other words, there is far less pressure in the relationship.

One last important part of the 100% solution is that sometimes it is more important to be happy than it is to be right. In some situations, it might be difficult for both people to make the first move or take the first step.

While one person might be right and the other dead wrong, being able to put that aside and be the positive force in resolving things can be the difference in saving the relationship or parting ways.

The 100% solution enables people in all kinds of relationships to get through more problems and situations and allows them to build stronger and more stable relationships. People with this kind of attitude are concerned more with the overall health of the relationship and not as much about themselves and who is right or wrong. So instead of placing blame, they search for solutions. Instead, of holding a grudge, they work on solutions. The result is almost always a stronger and more positive relationship with a foundation of trust and security.

Treat Her Right

At the root of every relationship lies the way both people treat each other. That basis will either help make the relationship stronger or blast it apart. Each person has the responsibility to treat the other person properly and with dignity and respect. After all, you cannot feel safe and secure in any relationship if both people are not fully committed to treating each other properly.

The other important reason for treating each other right is the establishment of trust. This trust is what permits both of you to be vulnerable with each other and share your innermost feelings and emotions. No intimate or romantic relationship can survive without this sharing of feelings, emotions and dreams.

Even though this is a basic right or expectation in a relationship, you would be shocked to discover how many people treat their partner poorly or even worse.

So by making it a priority to treat your partner like they are entitled to be treated you will almost immediately place yourself at a higher level than others she might have dated or been in a relationship with.

How your partner perceives you is very important. Though perceptions are not always accurate or even based on truth or fact, they are the reality in the mind of your partner. So it makes little difference if how your partner feels is justified or not. It is their version of reality and you must deal with that perception.

People do not always deal with emotions and feelings in a rational manner. Because of this, it is best to treat people in such a manner that your good intentions will come shining through and leave no doubt that you are a good person who honestly cares for your partner. This kind of feeling is important because it will help your partner get through the tough times that lie ahead in any relationship.

With this in mind, here are a few tips and guidelines as they pertain to how you should treat your partner:

Dignity & Respect

Everyone, and I mean everyone, deserves to be treated with dignity and respect.

Even if people treat you poorly it does not justify treating them poorly in response. Your treatment of every human being, whether they are your partner or not, should be based on dignity and respect. If a person treats you poorly you should either leave the relationship or help them work through the situation. That is a better response than bringing yourself down to their level. Discretion is always the better alternative.

That means being patient with them during times of stress and supporting their views and opinions when necessary. It means respecting their values and morals and not putting down someone for believing something you do not believe.

It also means allowing people to be themselves around you and not making fun or ridiculing someone because they made a mistake or had done something wrong. People do make mistakes and your partner should feel that they can make a mistake, or admit to a mistake, in your presence and not be made fun of or judged by you.

Never Raise your Hand

Physical attacks or violence against a woman is never appropriate. It is always better to exit the situation when tempers flare or get out of hand.

Physical responses or violence is an abuse of trust and is usually considered a deal breaker when it comes to continuing the relationship. Once you hit your partner a piece of that trust leaves and is never regained.

If your partner treats you badly, or does something bad to you, or even if they get physical with you, turn the other cheek and exit the situation immediately. Do NOT retaliate or escalate the situation. If the physical attack was severe, or if was life threatening in nature you may wish to contact the authorities so that others are not placed at risk either.

Physical violence, whether a single incident or a pattern of abuse, is an indication that this response is part of your partners character and it is something you must think very strongly about as far as the future of the relationship is concerned. No person, whether male or female, should subject themselves to physical attacks from their partner. There is no relationship that worth keeping if it involves any kind of abuse.

Make Her Feel Special

One difference between a friend and a boyfriend is that a boyfriend should make her feel special.

You can have many friends but just one mate or spouse. That "chosen one" should make you feel needed, loved, appreciated and treasured. It is not enough to know she is special; you need to show her she is special!

You can do that in a number of ways but acknowledging her place in your life is a great way to start. Let her know you appreciate her being in your life. Let her know your life is better because she is a part of it. You might think that sounds a bit corny but it is very important to your partner.

All romantic relationships, especially in the beginning contain some insecurity or uncertainty. Your partner will wonder if you really like her or love her. She will wonder if she is good enough or sexy enough for you. She may wonder if there are other women in your life and, if so, how she measures up. In other words, she has the same questions and misgivings that you probably have as well.

Because of this, a boyfriend who understands those feelings and takes steps to address them and reassure their partner is a great boyfriend. It shows that you care about your partner and that it is important the she feel at ease and secure in your arms. It shows you value her emotional state and how she feels about you and your relationship.

There are a ton of guys in this world who are either clueless when it comes to this or that just don't care.

Women know this and are looking for men who are not afraid to show their feelings and address their partners feeling as well. At the very least it call comes down to treating people with dignity and respect. If you have each other's feelings and best interests at heart almost everything else falls in line.

Respect Her Friends & Family

This is something a lot of guys miss the boat on. They treat their partners great but not their friends and family. If you stop and think about this for a minute, it really makes no sense. Especially when you stop and realize that you are one of her friends as well!

Friends and relatives share a common bond with people. Something within them strikes a chord in their minds. They have certain things in common. They like some of the same things and they share certain likes and dislikes. Their emotional make up is usually similar as well. Because of this, when you dismiss one of their friends or relatives, you are dismissing part of them at the same time.

One of the cardinal rules when it comes to sales is to never put down something the customer owns.

That is because people buy things that they like and when you put down something they own it is like putting the customer down at the same time. While it is not my intention to compare people with possessions, the response is the same.

So make an effort to get along with her friends and family. Include them in social outings. Throw a party and invite some of her friends and family and not just yours. You really do need to make an effort to fit in with her family and social life. While a relationship could succeed without this interaction, it is much easier when everyone gets along.

When you can become part of her life and allow her to be part of yours, your relationship will become deeper and stronger. Never make her choose between you and her friends or family. This is bound to cause resentment and most of the time she will not choose you! So get to know her friends and family and work hard to establish a good relationship with those people as well.

Make Her Your # 1

Would it make you feel all nice and fuzzy knowing that in your partner's eyes you are a very special #4 person in their lives?

You know, right behind her best friend, her boss and her hair stylist? Off course it wouldn't. You want to be thought of as being #1 and she wants exactly the same thing.

That means making her a priority in your life. It means letting her know she is #1 not just by saying so but by the things you do as well. It means telling her she is important to you. It means making her the priority in your life when it comes to your time and social life. It means going to her family gathering when all the guys are going to the big playoff game this Saturday night.

No one likes to be thought off as an afterthought or a last resort. If you place spending time with the guys above spending time with her, that is going to be a problem. If you wait to see if something better comes along before committing to doing something with her that is going to cause a problem as well.

That does not mean that you have to dedicate all your time and resources to your partner. We all need our private time and time with friends. But if that is your priority, then you need to have your priorities re-evaluated. Communicate with each other and let each other know how important you are to each other. Make each other your #1 priority and make sure you both know it!

Be Open & Honest

Honesty is a word that makes some guys shiver and shake in their boots. But the fact is, if you cannot be open and honest with your partner then there is little hope for the relationship. If you want to be a great boyfriend, be honest with her. Let her know what is on your mind. If it might be something she doesn't want to hear, be gentle. But be honest.

Relationships built on lies will soon begin to crumble. You cannot place lie upon lie and not have things catch up with you. Your partner will discover you are lying at some point and whatever trust and security she had with the relationship will be gone. Though some might eventually come back, it will likely never be the same in the future.

Express feelings honestly as well. Part of the growth of any relationship is learning how the other person feeling about different things in life. If we don't share how we truly feel, our partners will never really know who and what we really are.

Sometimes honesty is not the easiest thing to do especially when it comes to someone we care very deeply for. After all, we don't want to hurt their feelings and we don't want to do anything that might damage the relationship either. But even when something negative has to be shared, any short term anger or damage will be far less than behaving or acting in a lie.

As we said, be open, be honest and be gentle. That is the only way any relationship can stand the test of time.

The Golden Rule

Sometimes it is difficult to know what to do in any given situation. You might wonder what to say, what to do, how to act, or how to handle a situation that comes your way. Since we are all different and have different likes and dislikes, there is no one cookie cutter approach to life. So the best advice we have to give you is to abide by the "golden rule".

The golden rule says that we should treat everyone like we would like them to treat us. In other words, if we would like to have something happen to us, that is what we should offer to the other person. Nowhere is this truer than when it comes to romantic or intimate relationships.

Think about one thing for a minute. If you are in a romantic relationship with someone, you are usually closer to that person than most everyone else in your life. That is because you probably have several things in common and have pretty much the same likes and dislikes. In fact, in many ways you are identical.

So if you are identical in many ways then it stands to reason that what you would like and what your partner would like will be very close. So if you find yourself in a certain situation and you know how you would like to see things turn out then your partner would probably like to see them turn out the same way. It will at least give you a start when it comes to figuring out what to do!

Be Understanding

Sometimes it is not enough to allow people to be who they are and support them as they make their own decisions. You not only have to be supportive you must be understanding as well. Even when you do not necessarily agree with what someone does or says, you need to make an attempt to understand your partner at all times.

It is tough going through life and sometimes we need the support and understanding of those who we allow to be close to us. We need to be able to come home to an understanding partner who will listen to our problems and issues and understand what we are going through. In other words, we need someone to talk to when times get stuff.

Not only that, we need people around us who understand why we want the things we want and why we dream of the things we dream of. In simpler terms, we need people who understand who we are and why we are that way. We need people who are not just content to know things about us but also want to understand the "why" behind those things.

Understanding certain things about our partners requires a deeper understanding of the person and being willing to make that effort is something very important to your partner. It might be easier to find someone who will support you in life but finding someone who totally understands you can be much more difficult and therefore much more special.

Know what is Important to Her

If you really want to win her heart, make the effort to find out as much about her as you can. Ask her questions, find out what is important to her and why. Find out what she looks for in other people. Look at her family and friends and examine those relationships. What makes her happy or sad? What things does she value most in other people? What are her hopes and dreams? What touches her heart and her soul?

Knowing these things helps us figure out what we can do to endear ourselves to her. This is not to say we should be someone we are not, but sometimes a simple thought or gesture can make a world of difference to her. If you know something means a lot to her, and it means something to you as well, that can give you something to concentrate your efforts on.

Keep in mind that the strength of the relationship depends on how well it meets the needs of both people. If you know what is important to your partner and are willing and able to provide more of that to them, then your overall relationship will be stronger and more rewarding and fulfilling for both of you.

Know the Things She is Sensitive About

Not everyone processes emotions and situations exactly the same. We all react differently because some things mean more to us than other things. Sometimes the reactions will be over the top because there is strong emotional response to something that really hits home for us.

Make an effort to recognize the things she is sensitive about or has a more pronounced reaction to. This can give you valuable insight into understanding how you should approach or react to certain situations.

The more you can understand why someone reacts a certain way the better you will be able to handle those responses when they come around.

All of this comes down to communication and awareness. The more you become aware of her feelings and responses the more effective you will be able to communicate with each other and comfort each other as well.

Don't Just Know, Understand

Most guys are content with just knowing something. For them it is enough to know that their girlfriend is overly sensitive or emotional. But they never take the time or make the effort into trying to understand just why that is.

It is like being taught something in school but never asking for an explanation. Most knowledge does you little good unless you can find a way to use that knowledge in your life. When it comes to relationships, understanding your partner on a deeper level will enable you to become a more sensitive and supportive person.

Sometimes this might entail asking your partner questions about why they react like they do.

Approach these questions from a positive point of view and make sure your partner is aware that these questions are being asked so that you can become more informed and not because you are criticizing her for anything. Take it slow and don't make her feel that she is being interrogated. Let her know you are trying to understand certain things and would like to know more. If you can do this in the right manner it will be received very positively.

Fight Fair

Into every relationship a little rain must fall. There will be fights and disagreements and some of them might be very intense. You cannot eliminate them but you can minimize their occurrence and their impact on your relationship. Your efforts should be on handling these situation effectively and positively so the relationship can move on in a positive manner.

Fighting fair refers to having boundaries and limits on what can be done and said during fights. A perfect example of this would be an understanding that no physical attacks will be tolerated. A lesser rule might be to agree that you will never use profane language or that you will never go to bed mad at each other.

Another rule should also be to treat each other with dignity and respect even when you are fighting. This can be hard when emotions are running hot and words are being said before you really thought about what you were saying.

Another rule should be that you do not "stockpile" things to be used time and time again during fights or disagreements. Once something is discussed and resolved it should not be brought up again unless it directly is relevant to the current situation. For example, if your partner cheated on you in the past and she has done so again, it would be fair to bring up the past event.

But if she cheated on you in the past and she was late for dinner last night and didn't call you, it would not be appropriate for you to say you thought she was late because she was cheating on your again like she had done before. That accomplishes nothing except to inflame emotions already running high.

Your comments and actions should be directed towards positively resolving the situation. It should not be about who is right and who is wrong, but instead what can be done right now to make things better. If you can show your partner that your focus is not on placing blame but in making everything better, that attitude will be very much appreciated.

That is where understanding is important. With every disagreement or fight there is a clash of attitudes and viewpoints. If you make an attempt to understand why someone did what they did or thinks what they think, then some of the anger you have might disappear. Knowing the reasons behind something can make it easier to process and deal with. It is when we take something at face value and not make any attempt to understand it that we often run into trouble.

Trust Her

One of the quickest and easiest ways to destroy a relationship before it gets started is to be jealous or suspicious of your partner. Usually this type of activity comes from insecurity but it can also come from fear of losing someone who is really important to you. In those cases even well intentioned behavior can result in frightening your partner away.

Trust is very important in every relationship but it is even more critical when it comes to a romantic or intimate relationship. The ability to feel safe and secure with each other is one of the cornerstones of a solid and rewarding relationship.

First and foremost, both partners need to be 100% honest with each other. Every lie is a potential source of distrust and suspicion.

The feeling is that if they lied once that can lie twice or more and it is hard to find fault with that kind of reasoning. The fact is that if you lie and you get caught, things might never be the same. So first and foremost, be honest and open with each other. Not part of the time or most of the time but all of the time. Be open, be honest and be gentle when called for. Never lie or intentionally mislead or hide things from your partner.

After that, here are a few things you should never do when it comes to trust:

Don't Be Jealous

If you take one thing away from this chapter is that you should avoid all attempts to be a jealous boyfriend. Jealous people are usually not received very well and relationships with jealous people usually run their course in a very short time.

Jealous people are not trusting people either. Despite their efforts the level of trust goes way down instead of way up. Both people in the relationship need s their own space to grow. When that is taken away, the relationship dies.

Don't Suffocate Her

Every person needs their space. No matter how much you are in love and no matter how close you might be, everyone needs some time on their own and their own personal space. When one partner does not allow the other to have their own life and tries to dominate every waking hour, the relationship suffers.

There needs to be a level of trust and respect between both partners. They need to trust each other when they are apart like they do when they are together. They need to have a certain level of confidence in their partner as well. If one partner is so insecure that they must be with their partner every waking moment, the other partner will soon develop resentment towards their partner. Once this happens, the relationship can be doomed.

Don't Look at Her Phone

Today's phones hold a wealth or personal information in addition to phone numbers. There are address books, text messages, pictures and other information that is intended to be private. Don't look into her phone to see who she has been calling or who is in her address book.

Don't look to see if that old boyfriend is still in her address book or whether she deleted the pictures of them that she had taken 5 years ago.

This is none of your business and even if those items are still there does not mean they are still in contact or that there are any leftover feelings. It could be that she just forgot or that the pictures represent pleasant memories for other reasons than having her old boyfriend in them.

Don't look into her Social Media Accounts

For the same reasons as we just discussed, stay out of her Facebook and Social media accounts. Stop looking at her pages to see who is contacting her or what she is saying. Even though this information is out there for everyone to see doesn't mean you should be looking at these pages regularly.

This kind of digital talking can be kind of creepy. It sends the wrong message to your partner. It lets them know you don't trust them or that you are an insecure person at heart. You want to appear confident in yourself and your place in her life. That is an attractive feeling in the eyes of your partner. Your partner wants someone who is confident and secure not someone who feels the needs to check up on her behind her back.

Don't Sneak Around or Follow Her

One thing you should never do is sneak around and follow your partner to see where she goes and what she does. Not only do you run the risk of her seeing you, you also run the risk of her friends or family seeing you and that can create a whole other set of problems for you.

This kind of activity is called stalking and it is illegal in most states. This is not to say your partner will call the police on you but they will not usually react very positively to being followed or stalked. They want to be trusted and they want to have their privacy and personal life respected as well.

This is another activity that labels you as being very insecure and that is not a very flattering way to be looked at. You want to be seen as someone confident in himself and secure in the relationship. You want to be viewed as strong and not weak. Very few women want to be in a relationship with a weak man.

Don't Check Up on Her!

Never try to check on your partner by asking her friends or family members questions about what she does or where she goes. Not only does this place those relationships in jeopardy but you can be sure those questions will find their way back to your partner. That never goes over very well!

Don't question your partner on where she was, what she did or when she got home either. That is condescending and none of your business. She has her own life and does not have to answer to you as far as what she does or doesn't do when you're not there!

If you have suspicions about your partner and really feel it is critical that you get some questions answered, then ask her directly. But be aware that those questions are not likely to be received very well and just asking them might place the relationship in danger or turmoil. But there might be situations where you do need to get something out in the open and in those cases the question might really need to be asked.

Communicate Well

Guys, you might not like to hear this but one thing men usually have problems with is our communication skills. We either don't want to know, don't know how to find out or don't know what to do with the information once we get it. Emotions can be difficult to deal with and sometimes it is easier to ignore them than confront them.

It is often said that the words "We need to talk" strike fear in the hearts of most men. That is because those words are usually the prelude to an unpleasant conversation. Men and women are different and we deal with things differently. That means that men sometimes think they are doing the right thing only to find out they were 100% wrong. Women, on the other hand, feel 100% right in how they see things and feel that we should just see them the same way. When we don't, it hits the fan.

The only way to limit these kinds of problems is to develop great communication skills. Being able to communicate with your partner means that more things are discussed and less is left to interpretation.

But communication is more than just talking. It is about talking and listening and hearing what isn't expressed in just the words we hear. In fact, less than 10% of what we say is in the words we use to say it. The rest comes from body language, the tone of the voice and the emotions behind the words. In some cases the same words can have opposite meanings depending on how those words were spoken.

So we not only have to hear the words we have to see them and experience them as well. So with that in mind, here are a few pointers when it comes to communicating effectively with your partner:

Be Honest

You will see this repeated often throughout this book but it is especially important when it comes to communicating effectively. Whenever you talk to your partner you need to be open and honest. Don't tell your partner what you think she wants to hear unless that is what you really want to say.

If something is bothering you, pick the right time and place to discuss it openly and honestly. This is the only way your partner can understand what you want or need from the relationship. If you are never honest with your partner, things will never get resolved and the relationship cannot grow or flourish.

When you lie, or when you are not fully open and honest, you can send the wrong signals to your partner and that can make problems worse instead of better. While sometimes being honest might not be very easy, in the long run it is the best thing to do. If you need to say something negative, or if you risk hurting your partner's feelings by being honest, find a gentle and compassionate way of doing so.

Your goal should be to be honest in as positive way as you possible can. You might not believe it at the time but your partner will appreciate a partner who is open and honest. Most of us have been lied to or deceived by others and when we find someone who is really honest with us all of the time that is special.

Balance Conversations

I hate to break it to you but no one is so interesting that they should do all the talking all the time.

You might be a really interesting person but hearing you talk about yourself for an entire evening is not the way most women want to spend their evening. They should be the focus and not you. This is especially important at the beginning of the relationship. You should want to hear about her day, what happened at work and other things.

Try to balance the conversation so that she does at least half the talking, hopefully a little more than half, and make sure the focus is on her and not you. There will be time for you to talk about yourself but make the focus on her and what she feels is important. But also keep in mind that she might try to balance the conversation so that you talk more for the same reasons. Don't obsess over who talks the most, just make sure it is at least somewhat balanced. Ask leading questions designed to get her talking. Ask her about her day or her hobby or something she would be willing or even excited to talk about.

Your partner will appreciate your interest and attention and at the same time you will be learning more and more about who your partner is and what she likes and dislikes. It is one of those situations where making your partner feel appreciated will also help you out in the long run as well.

When the guy balances the conversation they are telling their partner that they matter to them. They feel important and valued. That makes their partner appreciate them more at the same time. Relationships are all about mutual respect and making sure that both partners get to share the conversation is just something that should always be done.

Really Listen

When people listen, they rarely listen effectively. They might hear the words but not hear the meaning behind those words. Or they might hear the words but not fully process them. Sometimes we are distracted by things going on around us or in our own minds that we miss important information that is staring us right in the face.

When we listen we should do our best to tune out distractions. Pay attention to what your partner is telling you. If you are reading a book, put it down. If the game is on TV, turn it off or look away. Let your partner know they are your focal point and not something or someone else.

Stop thinking about other things as well. Sometimes we are thinking so hard about what we are going to say next we neglect to hear what is being said at that moment.

That sometimes results in use saying the wrong thing or jumping to the wrong conclusions. Either way, concentrate on what your partner is saying so you hear everything.

Not only that, pay attention to the emotions behind the words. We often say something in anger that we really don't mean so we need to be aware of emotions while we are speaking. When we are angry we fail to communicate accurately and effectively so it makes sense to try and calm each other down first and then talk things over. The more rational and calm we are the more accurately we choose our words and message.

Also "listen" to the body language of your partner. If their stance is aggressive that conveys that they are upset or mad even though their voice might not reflect that. In some situations body language is kind of an "early warning" system that can give you some insight into the situation before it is evident in words or emotions.

All of these methods of listening help you get more information about what your partner is really saying to you. This enables you to make better and more accurate decisions and have an overall more accurate and complete understanding of the situation and conversation. All of this can be yours if you just learn to listen.

Compromise

Communication is not about who is right and who is wrong. It is about the free flowing exchange of information and ideas. Excellent communication occurs when both people are relaxed and not afraid to speak what is on their mind. That means that it is important that we be able to compromise on things as we communicate.

When people are assessed with blame, or even when they think they are being blamed they tend to shut down. They get defensive and that hurts the communication process. People tend to get defensive when confronted and this can lead to guarded conversations or no communications at all.

Communication and compromise mean that it is more important to be happy than right. Keep the lines of communication open by being non-confrontational whenever possible. That does not mean that someone should be given a free pass to do anything wrong. What it does mean is that we should discuss issues and situations and resolve them not just blame someone for them. It also means letting the little stuff go once in a while. Those little things often are not worth the time and effort to discuss. After all, if you have an otherwise perfect partner who doesn't always put their dirty clothes in the laundry; is that really such a big deal?

Share Your Feelings with Her

If you want to be considered a special and great boyfriend, share your feelings with her. Allow yourself to be vulnerable. Talk about what makes you happy or sad. Let her know what is important to you. Encourage her to do the same with you. Try and get to know each other on a deeper and more intimate level.

Your partner will appreciate that you feel comfortable and secure enough with her to let her into your world. That shows her that she has a special place in your heart and that you want to make her a larger part of your life. Most men feel awkward talking about their emotions or feelings. This can make their partners insecure because they want to become a larger part of their partner's life but are not allowed to do so.

Share Your Dreams with Her

As your relationship proceeds, share your dreams with her. Tell her where you see yourself 5, 10, 25 years down the road. Let her know what you want to do, what you want to achieve and where you see yourself living.

This not only let's her become part of your inner life but it also shows her what is in your heart.

After all, you want someone who is going to help you turn your dreams into reality. If she has different thoughts or dreams that might mean this is the wrong partner for you and it is better to find that out now rather than later.

But if you share those dreams, and encourage her to share hers with you, you will find out that you are even more compatible and that can add depth and excitement into the relationship. The result is that the two of you become closer and your relationship becomes stronger. You can proceed and start helping each other turn your hopes and dreams into reality. Isn't that what a relationship should be all about?

Compromise

Relationships are all about compromise. No relationship can possibly succeed when one person calls all the shots, makes all the decisions and does everything that they want. Successful relationships exist when both partners get at least some control over what happens within the relationship. It's all about give and take.

No matter how much two people might be alike, there will always be difference over what each of you will like or dislike. Your partner might want to go and see the latest "chick flick" while you want to see the latest action movie all the guys are talking about. If you want to score some points with your lady, go to the chick flick.

Being in a relationship also means sometimes doing something you really don't want to do.

You do these things to make your partner happy. You do them because you know she appreciates it and because you want to make her happy. Chances are she will want to do the same for you at times so it all boils down to a little give and take.

Here are a few tips when it comes to compromising so that both of you get as much of what you want from your relationship:

Give Each Other the Most of What You Want

Relationships are not about winning or losing. There should never be a clear cut winner in every situation in a relationship unless that is the goal of both partners. For example, if it is your birthday, then it is fine to allow yourself to get everything you want on that day. But for every other day, you should strive to give each of you the most of what you want.

This is called a win-win resolution and it should be the goal of every person in a relationship. You should strive to make reasonably certain that the needs of both of you are being addressed each and every day. Always factor in her needs and expectations. Try and give her as much of what she wants as possible while still allowing yourself to be happy as well.

When you have a disagreement or fight, don't try to adopt a winner take all mentality in getting it resolved. Instead, look for a way for both of you to get something positive from the resolution. In some cases being happy is more important than being right. Always give some thought as to how you can arrive at a resolution that will help both of you, not just you.

One additional benefit of approaching things in this manner is that when your partner sees that you are trying to give her what she wants she will be more receptive to what you are trying to do. In any negotiation when both parties get some of what they want they find it much easier to reach an agreement. Relationships are a constant form of negotiation and the win-win approach is almost always the best approach to take.

Let Her Choose What to Do

The days where the man chooses where to go and what to do are long over. Today what the woman wants is equally important and you should feel that way as well. So let her decide what to do or where to go once in a while. Even when it's your turn to pick, give some thought as to what she might like as well.

If there are two things you would like to do or two movies you would like to see, try and figure out which one she would enjoy more and choose that one. This way both of you get what you want and both of you are happy. Always remember that your goal must always be for BOTH of you to have fun and enjoy your time together.

Always Think of Her Needs

Like we said, relationships get better when both people enjoy the time they spend together. To help you become a great boyfriend, always think of her needs when deciding what the two of you are going to do that night or over the weekend. Your goal should be to create the best time for both of you. That doesn't mean she gets to do everything she wants all the time. What it does mean is that you should always factor in what she wants in your decision.

For example, if there are two important playoff games on TV next weekend try and balance things out so that you do something she likes when the games aren't on. That might be going to her favorite restaurant or bringing in her favorite takeout food to eat during the games. If there are a few hours between the games consider taking a walk in the park or doing something else she enjoys. This way both of you get to do something you enjoy and both of you are happy.

It is amazing how different your decisions will be when you make an effort to consider what your partner might want to do as well. It is all about being considerate to your partner like they are considerate to your needs.

Let Her Pick the Radio Station or TV Show

If you want to endear yourself to your girlfriend, why not have a day or a weekend where your partner chooses what you will do? Let her pick the movie or TV shows you watch. Let her pick the restaurant or the activities the two of you will do.

If you REALLY want to knock her off her feet, YOU design the perfect day or weekend and plan all the things that you know SHE loves to do. Go to that movie she wants to see. Take her to her favorite restaurant for dinner. Throw a party and invite a lot of her friends. In other words, pamper her with all the things you just know she will love and enjoy! Chances are she will return the favor at some point with a special time for you as well.

What is really special about doing this is not so much the things you do or the places you go. It is that you took the time and initiative to think about what she would like to do. It shows you care about her and it shows her that she is important to you.

As for your pleasure and enjoyment, that comes from seeing her have such a good time with you. Everything else is secondary.

Be Supportive

One of the most important things you can do in your relationship is being supportive towards your partner whenever she needs it. You might not agree with what she is doing or what she wants but if it is important to her you should support her in her efforts.

Everyone needs support as they go through their lives. When times get tough, or when important decisions need to be made, we look to those closest to us for help and support. If that support is not there when we expect it to be, that can cause problems. Being supportive towards the ones we love is a very important part of our lives.

Support is also more than telling someone you are behind them. It means doing and saying the things necessary to make that person feel better about themselves on a daily basis.

It means giving them the strength they need to follow through on their commitments and efforts. It means helping them when help is needed and being there for them when they need someone to lean on.

Commitment also means helping her make decisions and giving your input and assistance whenever needed or asked for. It also means being understanding when other things keep her away from you or cause her to temporarily place other things in her life ahead of you. Though this can sometimes be very difficult, it is something you need to do whenever the situation calls for it. You simply cannot be supportive and selfish at the same time.

Here are some ways you can be supportive to your partner and help your relationship grow:

Compliment Her Sincerely

Everyone likes to be complimented. Everyone likes to hear nice things said about them. It makes us feel good, it makes us feel appreciated and it adds value to who we are in our minds. Compliments also give us confidence and strength and help us develop belief in ourselves at the same time.

For most men, compliments are usually about physical appearance. "You look great tonight" or "That dress is very beautiful" are some of the most common compliments we give our ladies. But some of the best compliments are not about who our partners look. A compliment such as "I am so proud of you" or "You did such a great job on that project" are more sincere and more appreciated than compliments about physical attractiveness. (Although be sure to give those compliments as well!)

Be honest with your compliments but do not hesitate to tell her something nice whenever it is called for. Tell her the meal she cooked was wonderful. Tell her you appreciate her in your life. Tell her you appreciate the things she does for you. If there is something you really think is special about her, let her know. These are the compliments that will melt her heart and make you even more special and wonderful in her eyes.

Be Interested in Her Life

Your partner is more than just a person. She has a life and experiences that help make her who and what she is. You need to be interested not only in her as a person but in her life as well. Ask her about her work, her hobbies and every other part of her life.

Become part of her family and circle of friends. Don't isolate her from her friends and family. Invite them into your relationship. They are part of who she is and they should become part of who you are as well. Relationships mean letting each other into our existing lives in addition to creating a new life for the two of you. Showing interest into the rest of her life with help you become closer and tighter as a couple.

Be Sympathetic

We all make mistakes and we all have things that don't work out the way we planned. When that happens to your partner you need to be right there to comfort her and become sympathetic. You need to listen to her problems and listen to her vent her anger and frustration.

Being in a relationship means taking the good with the bad. It means sharing the good times and being there to help pick up the pieces during the bad times. It means being part of the solution and not part of the problem. It means being the person she comes to for help, compassion and support. If you can be that person, your relationship will flourish.

Protect Her

Though a lot of things have changed over the last 50 years, women still like a man who will stand up for her and protect her when she needs it. That means making her feel safe and secure when she is with you. It means placing her own safety and well-being ahead of your when the situation calls for it.

Being protective doesn't mean you have to fight all her battles or that she is helpless. Instead it means being aware of what is going on in her life and helping her remain safe and secure. It means keeping your eyes and ears open and protecting her when certain things might happen.

Stand Up for Her When Others are Against Her

These days a lot of people love to criticize or put down other people. Usually these people do not have the guts or the integrity to do this face to face. Instead they do it behind the persons back. When n this happens, and you become aware of it, do not sit idly by and let those statements or attacks go unchallenged. Stand up for your partner and make it known that you do not tolerate people making unfounded accusations or attacks on your friends.

If this happens when the two of you are together, stand up for her as well.

Allow her to respond at first but if it becomes obvious that she needs outside help, step in. Support her in front of others and let it be known that an attack on her is the same as an attack on you. She will appreciate the gesture and support. Just make sure you allow her to make the first move or response so you don't make her appear weak and defenseless. (But don't wait too long either!)

Make Time for Her Even When it's Not Convenient

We all have our own commitments and obligations as well. Sometimes our schedules can get really crazy and become jam-packed with all kinds of things. But even in those situations, try and make time for her in your life. Explain to her that you are really busy this week or at a particular time but make her aware that you have carved out some time just for the two of you.

Keep in mind that when you are too busy for your partner that you are in fact telling her that something or someone else is more important to you than she is. That is never a message that you want to send anyone let alone your partner.

The key is to make an honest effort to set aside some time for the two of you. Even it is only enough time to grab a quick lunch during a marathon week at work

. Just make the effort to see each other even during those tight times.

The second thing is to make sure you communicate the reasons why you are so busy. Let her know about that huge project due at the end of the month or that you have a big test or other obligation at the end of the month or whenever the time frame might be. Let her know these things so she is aware of what is going on in your life and doesn't start imagining that you are seeing someone else or avoiding her for some reason.

Like everything else in life, good and accurate communication and treating people properly will help you through those busy times and allow you to keep the relationship intact and strong.

Do the Things SHE Thinks are Important

Here is a good rule of thumb to go by in any romantic relationship. If it is important to your partner it should be important to you. Take an active interest in the things she feels are important and worthwhile to you. If she volunteers at a local charity, consider accompanying her once or twice a month. If she is active in a group, try to be active with her.

The more you can align with each other's life the closer and stronger you will become.

This does not mean you have to join or share every experience or that you have to do things you don't believe in or support. But at least give it a try and see how it goes. Just doing that will send a positive message to your partner that you care about her and the things in her life.

Be Her Refuge in Life

Everyone needs someplace to go when they are down and out. The need someplace and someone they can rely on no matter what. Whether something bad happened to them or they did something wrong does not matter. What does matter is that there's someone they can rely on to provide support and consolation when it's needed most.

Just knowing that she can come to you and you will support her when she needs it no matter what can be a tremendous relief and comfort to her even though she may never need it. Your responsibility as her partner means that you are ALWAYS there for her to fall back on. You are always there to help her pick up the pieces, reassure her and help her get back on her feet and move on.

If you can be that person, then let her know that. Be there when she needs it and help her deal with life's bad moments. Help her learn from her mistakes and failures. We all make mistakes and we all have failures. It is what we do when those things happen that separate the successful from the rest of us. Help her be successful and help her grow. She will appreciate your being there for her and helping her when she needs it most.

Notice Things About Her

This one is a quick hitter but it is still a very important part of the boyfriend experience. Whenever your partner changes something or does something, be sure to be aware of it and acknowledge it. Don't let her think you didn't notice and never assume that she knows that you noticed. Be upfront, acknowledge what you have noticed and compliment her.

There is not a guy alive who has forgotten to acknowledge a new hairstyle or a new dress or a new color or nail polish.

For guys, those things are not all that important because we don't worry about those things personally. We don't paint our nails and we don't change hairstyles. Most of us have had the same hairstyle since Junior High school. To be honest, none of those things make our top 10 list of important things.

But to our partners, sometimes those thing matter a great deal. If your partner cares for you she might spend extra time getting ready for your date. She may get a new manicure, change her hairstyle and buy a new dress because she wants to look nice for you. She wants you to be proud of her and she wants to look her best.

When you fail to acknowledge her effort that is like telling her what she did made no difference at all. It's like everything she did made no impression on you. Even more important, it shows that you really don't pay much attention to how she looks or what she does. Either way, the result is that your partner will be disappointed with you because you didn't notice.

Make an effort to look for subtle changes. Comment on her new hairstyle, her new nails or that new dress she bought. Make sure she is aware that you noticed and that you approve. But at the same time, be very careful because some comments can be taken the wrong way.

For example, it might not be a good idea to ask your partner if she has gained a few pounds. Mentioning that just could result in you winding up in the emergency room trying to have a foreign object removed from your body! The same applies for letting her know that the change she just made makes her look so much younger! That means you thought she looked much older before. Not a good thing to say or bring up.

All comments should be positive in nature and intended to make your partner feel better about herself without giving any negative images at the same time. For example, if your partner has a new dress, tell her it looks nice on her. But leave it at that. Don't say "That dress is really nice. It's not all like the frumpy dresses you usually wear." That is what is known as a back handed compliment. Keep it simple and keep it honest.

If you notice that your partner has lost some weight, just tell her she looks very nice. Let her volunteer that she lost weight and then tell her you are proud of her. You might tell her that she looked wonderful before but better now. This gives her positive commentary not only on her new appearance but on how she looked before as well. That kind of compliment will be extremely well received!

Sometimes we might realize that something is different but we are not exactly sure what is different. After all, we are guys and we are notoriously clueless when it comes to certain things. But even in those situations you can just tell her that she looks wonderful. You might say something like "You look wonderful tonight" and just leave it at that. Then follow the conversation and see where it leads.

The bottom line is that we need to make an attempt to be more aware and observant when it comes to our partners. We need to be aware of changes in emotions and personality so we can understand when something is wrong. We need to be aware of physical changes so we can acknowledge those changes and provide feedback and support.

All of this is leading to just being respectful and aware of our partners and what is going on with them and their lives. This is exactly the same thing we would hope that they will do when it comes to us.

Make Her Better

As we go through life, hopefully we become better people. Life experiences help us become smarter and more adept at handling life's little situations and we hopefully become older, wiser and smarter. One of the important things we can do in any relationship is help our partners become better people. Notice I said HELP them and not FORCE them to become better people. This is not about making someone a different person or helping them become something they do not wish to become. It is all about helping them become better and better equipped to handle those things that life throws at us.

Making someone better means providing help and support to assist them in achieving their goals and dreams.

It means sacrificing your time and efforts into helping your partner get more out of her life. That might mean encouraging her to keep up her efforts when she feels it might not be worth it. It is all about letting your partner know that you believe she can be successful and that she is capable of accomplishing anything and everything she sets her mind to.

For example you might help your partner study for a test or let them know you are willing to help them in their efforts to get their degree. You might be enthusiastic about helping your partner create a new career or open her own business. Whatever your partner wants to do you should be right there to help and support her.

But sometimes you can make someone better by letting them know they are about to make a mistake or by pointing out why something might not be the great idea that it sounds like. This happens all the time. We get so close to something that we can almost taste it and anything that suggests it is not for us we refuse to hear or acknowledge. So sometimes you might make someone's life better by keeping them from making mistakes,

We can also help make our partners better by challenging them to do more or achieve more. The challenges should be positive in nature and we should not force or overly push someone to do anything.

But sometimes we just need someone to tell us we should do something or someone to say what we want to do is not foolish or stupid.

Your partner needs to see you as a positive influence in her life. She needs to see that since you entered her life that she has improved as a person and as a human being. She should see personal and emotional growth as a result of you being in her life. Though this is not a requirement by any means, but if your partner realizes that you are part of that success this will help your relationship get to the next level.

The easiest way to make someone better is to take your ideas from the comments she makes about her future. If she says she is thinking about starting her own business, or taking a new job across town, then you should be right there to not only let her know that it sounds like a great idea but that you are also 100% certain that she can do this if she tries.

Let her know that her reluctance is understandable as change is never something we greet enthusiastically. If she voices concerns or obstacles help her work through those things and place her concerns or fears at ease. For example, if she wants to take a few courses but that will mean little time to spend together, let her know you will use that time to do something you have meant to do.

Maybe you can take a course as well. Perhaps you might volunteer to walk her dog or do her shopping or look in on her parents while she is taking the course.

The whole idea is to play a positive role in her development. Allow her and encourage her to become better at whatever she wants to become better at. Place her needs and her future ahead of yours and encourage her even if it might take her away from you. I'm not saying this will always be easy. Sometimes it can be very hard. But always support your partner and give her every opportunity to become the person she really hopes to be.

If you can accomplish that you will have endeared yourself to her forever.

Here are a couple of things you might consider when it comes time to help your partner become a better partner and person:

Be a Part of Her Growth

Change is hard and if your partner wants to change and become better at something, try and make yourself part of that change. Help her do whatever she needs to do. Help make things easier on her. Be understanding and realize that change is difficult for some people. Be there to cheer her on and support her.

See if there are any ways that you can help her. Maybe you could try and do the same thing and support each other. If it is her passion why not try and make it yours as well? If she wants to join a gym and work out, join her. Not only will this help her achieve her goals it will allow you to share the time together and the process as well.

Encourage Her to Be and Do Better

Everyone needs some encouragement especially when you hit a roadblock or two along the way. Tell her you are proud of her. Even if her efforts take her away from you for a while, tell her you support her. Let her know you are in her corner all the way.

If you see any changes, let her know you see them. Make her aware that you notice the changes and are proud of her accomplishments. This will not only make her feel good but will motivate her to keep up her efforts and accomplish even more moving forward.

You should be her #1 fan and her biggest cheerleader. Make her success your success. Be excited for her. Let her know you are proud of what she is doing in her life. Sometimes her decisions will not be popular to others and she will look to you for validation and support.

Be Supportive of Her Choices

As we just said, sometimes our decisions are not popular with everyone. Whenever we try and change something someone stands to have their lives changed in the process. Maybe getting back to your education will take you away from your friends. Maybe changing jobs will make it harder for others to live their lives. But you must always realize that you have to live your life and not someone else's.

As part of a relationship, you may be called upon to place your needs above your own. Maybe your partner will need to do something that might hurt you in the process. Maybe she wants to go away for a while to take a class or get an education. She will naturally feel bad and nervous about how you will react.

In times like these you need to suck it up and let her know you support her. Tell her you will visit and call her often. Let her know you will be there when she gets back. In general, let her know the two of you will work things out so that she can follow her dreams or make her life better. That is just what people in healthy relationships do for each other.

Don't Force Change Upon Her

One thing about change is that you really have to want to change in order for you to give it your best efforts. You cannot change because someone else wants you to. You might try but if your heart isn't in it you will likely give up.

As far as your partner is concerned, you really shouldn't force any change upon her unless it is a matter of life or death. Ultimatums usually do not work and should be used as a last resort. It is almost always better to work through the issue and get your partner on board with whatever the change is going to involve.

That means being patient and supportive of her choices no matter what those choices might be. Unless they are dangerous or threaten her health, you need to be on-board. Voice your concerns and your opinions but always remember the decision must be hers and not yours. You are responsible for your life and behavior and she is responsible for here. While you might not like it, that's exactly how it must be.

Make Her Feel Better About Herself

The primary reason for any type of relationship is that the relationship makes both people feel better about themselves and their lives. That means both people feel that the presence of the other makes their lives better, richer and more fulfilling and rewarding. Without these feelings, there is little need for the relationship at all.

So it stands to reason that one of your primary goals should be to make your partner feel better about herself. You should make her feel better, more valuable and more desirable than she felt before you came on the scene. If you are not making her feel that way, there is something missing. Whenever someone notices something is missing in a relationship they begin to look elsewhere for it.

So it just makes sense to try and do the things that make your partner feel better about herself and your relationship. Here are a few things to think about when it comes to making anyone feel better about themself:

Be Her #1 Fan

As her boyfriend, you really need to become her biggest booster and her number one fan. You need to be the person who provides her with support, encouragement and praise. You should be the one who gives her strength and confidence. In other words, you need to be the one who inspires her to do more and feel better about herself.

Never miss an opportunity to tell her how great she is. Never miss an opportunity to give her a compliment. If you know she is insecure about something, do your best to reassure her and get her to believe in herself more.

Let Her Know How Much She Means to You

It's not enough to know how important she is to you or how much she means to you. What is important is that you make sure SHE knows it! Let her know how much she means to you. Don't take it for granted that she knows. Tell her every chance you get.

Thank her for the things she does for you. Tell her that you appreciate her and how happy you are that she is part of your life. Many guys are afraid to say these things because they might be afraid of commitment. But don't be afraid to share your feelings.

Just be careful not to do this too much or too early in the relationship as this might scare her off a little bit. But if the relationship has been established for a while, it is healthy to share your feelings between each other. The more you do this the easier it will come to both of you.

Stay with Her When She is Sick

It's easy to be with someone when everyone is happy and smiling. But it is another thing entirely when one of you is sick and has a runny nose, a fever and can't keep food in your body. That is the time when most guys will wish her well and tell her to call when she is feeling better.

Don't be that guy. Instead, come over and take care of her. Make her soup or a light meal or bring in some food she likes. Feed her if need be. Bring her hot tea of ice water. Place cool towels on her forehead and cater to her every need. Bring some movies she likes and just be with her.

Don't wait to be asked. Just come over and stay a while. If she asks you to leave, ask if you can stay. If she wants you to leave check back with her each day until she feels better. Everyone wants to be taken care of when they are sick and your partner is no different. This is one of the times when you can separate yourself from other guys she has known before.

Brag About Her to Others

It's perfectly fine to brag about her with your friends and other people. You can do this in front of her or when she is not present. After all, she is your partner and you should be proud of her. Never lose the opportunity to put in a good word about her with your friends and her friends. It's something a lot of guys don't do because they don't want to appear emotional. But a real man is not ashamed to admit their feelings and neither should you.

Value Her

Sometimes we start to take things for granted. The longer we know someone, the more we start to forget what made them so special in the first place. This doesn't mean with care for them less or love them less. It just means that we have become comfortable with them.

But we should make the time every so often to stop and remember what made her so special in the beginning.

Every so often stop and take time to remember what made her so special in the beginning. Remember her smile and her laugh and how she cares for you and everything else about you. The reason for doing this is because our brains treat things according to their perceived value. If you perceive something has a low value, you will not work very hard to keep it. But if you perceive someone to be extremely valuable to you then you will go to great lengths to keep that person in your life.

Above all, we don't want to forget or take for granted the things that made her so special and attractive in the first place. Always remembering those things will help you keep the magic in place in the relationship.

Be Affectionate & Loving

When we refer to being affectionate and loving some people automatically equate that with having sex or being intimate with your partner. While that may very well be the case, there is more to being affectionate and loving than the physical aspects of the relationship.

A romantic or intimate relationship almost always has a physical component. And I need to say right from the start that this physical component does not have to be sex. A physical component can refer to holding hands, kissing and other gestures. These things do not always have to lead to sex and in fact they shouldn't always lead in that direction. Being able to express your love and affection for your partner is an important part of the relationship.

But being affectionate is not always physical. You can show affection by showing her that you care. You can be affectionate by whispering little things in her ear or by giving an innocent hug or peck on the cheek. These are silent expressions of love and intimacy. Doing little things like this on a regular basis helps your partner feel loved, needed and appreciated. If the affection and intimacy leaves the relationship, it places a huge strain on what is left between you and your partner.

Here are some things to think about when it comes to showing affection and keeping the spark between the two of you alive and burning:

Show Affection Often

Never take affection for granted. Greet each other with a hug and a kiss. Say goodnight the same way. Hold her hand or walk with your arm around her. Even after things have gone on for a while, don't stop doing these things. Don't start taking intimacy or affection for granted. It's all right to act like teenagers again. In fact, it's encouraged!

Be Appropriate

There are proper times for intimate gestures.

Holding her and kissing her on the boardwalk on the beach is fine. Making out during Sunday Mass is usually frowned upon. Hugging and kissing on the couch in your apartment is wonderful. Making out at Grandma's with grandma and grandpa sitting across from you is not.

Everyone has their own comfort level when it comes to what they want to do and where they want to do it. Some people prefer not to show outward displays of affection in public places. If that is you or your partner, communicate that to each other. Otherwise, stay within accepted practices and don't make a spectacle of yourself or call attention to yourself.

Let Affection Stay Affection

Expressions of affection should not always lead to sex. If that is the case your partner might start resisting an innocent kiss or gesture because they are not in the mood for sex. Granted a kiss or hug can eventually lead to that in many relationships but it should not be the norm. Couples should be able to share a hug and a kiss without it leading to caresses and a pile of clothes on the floor.

This is one area where communication between both of you can play such an important role in your relationship. Establish boundaries and ground rules so you can share intimacy as well as affection without sending the wrong message to your partner. When there is confusion, stop and talk things through so there are no hurt feelings or frustration on either partner. When in doubt, talk it out!

Appreciate Her Looks

Your partner does things to make herself look nice for you. Acknowledge those things. Tell her she is beautiful. Tell her she looks sexy when it is appropriate. Don't take it for granted that she knows who you feel, TELL HER!

Give Her Presents

Send her flowers or surprise her by arriving with flowers when it's not her birthday or a special occasion. You don't have to go overboard and spend a lot of money. It is the gesture more than the flowers. The same applies to little gifts and presents. Bring her a small gift when it is not expected.

Anyone can bring a gift when it's a holiday or birthday, but the great boyfriend will bring one for no reason whatsoever. Just because he cares.

Isn't that a good reason right there?

Hold Her Hand in Public

Sometimes guys get a little embarrassed holding hands in public. Don't be one of those guys. Take her hand while walking and show her that you are proud to be seen in public holding her hand. It is a small gesture but one that can be very powerful in the mind of your lady.

Verbal Affection

Sometimes telling her how much you love her is just as effective as a nice romantic kiss. Be sure to tell her as well as show her how you feel. A well timed compliment or just telling her how much you care can really melt her heart. Try it and you'll see!

You can also leave her voicemails or messages on her answering machine just telling her you miss her or love her. Send her a text at lunch time telling her that you are thinking about her. Just be careful not to do this too much or too often as there can be a fine line between being affectionate and being a stalker!

Do Something Romantic

Take a carriage ride through the park. Take your shoes off and walk on the beach at night. Have an intimate dinner by candlelight. Whatever it might be that is special for the two of you make sure you keep doing it. Romance is more than verbal and physical. It lies in many different things and many different experiences. Try them all and never stop!

Whatever you do and whoever you do it, just make sure you keep on doing it. Never pass up the opportunity to bring the two of you together and express your love and feelings for each other. Even though you might not feel it, both of you need this to help keep your relationship alive and thriving.

Personality Traits for the Perfect Boyfriend

By now you should have a pretty good idea of what you should be doing and how you should be thinking. You understand where your focus should be and how you should treat your girlfriend. You understand the importance of making her feel wanted, needed and special. You also now understand that little things can have a huge impact.

Now that we have covered all of that, we thought we would take a step back and go over some personality traits that are generally looked for and appreciated by women when it comes to who they would like to be in a relationship with.

It doesn't mean you have to master each one, but you at least should be aware of them. The good thing is that you probably possess most of these anyway. But being aware of them might make you try a little bit harder or do certain things more often. So take a look and see where you might want to make some changes in your life to make yourself a better boyfriend.

Honesty

Women want someone who is honest and straight with them. They want someone they can trust and not someone who is going to play games with their lives and emotions. They want a man who is going to do what he says and can be taken at his word.

Most of all they want a man who is going to be fair and responsible and not cheat on them. Men would want the same thing so this is something everyone should understand.

Intelligent

You don't have to be a brain surgeon or a micro-biologist in order to get a great girl. But you can't be boring and uninteresting either. You should have a reasonable knowledge of what you are doing and what is going on in the world as well.

Since you will probably be going out with other people, it is important that you be able to hold your own in most conversations and be reasonably impressive in your ability to interact and communicate with others. If that is an area you feel needs improvement, you can start reading books and newspapers to become more aware of what is going on in the world.

If she has any particular interests, it might be a good idea to take out some books on that subject from the library so you can have something in common to talk about. She will appreciate the effort and you will have more the two of you can talk about together.

Open-Minded

Women like men who are not stuck in their ways and are open to trying new things and listen to new ideas or viewpoints. You do not have to accept those ideas or views but you should listen to them and not automatically dismiss them out of hand.

Trying new things is also important to most women. This way life can change as we get older and more comfortable with each other. Having someone willing to try something they never did before can be exciting for both of you. This will also help keep the relationship from getting stale or predictable.

Humorous

Life itself is far too serious and most people like to be around other people who make them smile and laugh every now and then. If you have a sense of humor then make sure you use it. Keep your comments and humor appropriate and remember that women and men find totally different things funny or amusing. So always remember who you are talking to.

While humor is important, remember that there are times when it is better to be serious. You must always balance your serious side with your funny side. Keep things light but recognize when humor is not appropriate. Balance is the key when it comes to humor.

Caring / Thoughtful

Women look for men who are caring and thoughtful. They want someone who is soft and tender and looks out for them. Men want the same things too but they are more important to women. Show your soft side and be caring and attentive.

Put yourself in her shoes and try and do the things that will make her feel special and appreciated. Try and think about her needs before your own and treat her like a queen. If you treat her in that manner she will treat you like a King!

Ambitious

Like it or not, the future of the relationship will depend on how both of you feel about how you and your partner will fare later in life. Your job at the supermarket might be OK for now but you cannot support a family mowing lawns or bagging groceries!

Women like to feel secure in their partner's ability to provide for her and the family later on in life. You don't need to have a great job now but you should be ambitious and inspire confidence as far as where you will be 10 or 20 years from now.

Spontaneous

Don't be predictable or a "stuffed shirt". Be adventurous and do things on a whim every now and then. Pick her up for a surprise date and plan something crazy every now and then. Have a great laugh at your expense as well.

In other words, make going out with you an interesting and never dull experience!

Good Listener

We covered this already but it bears repeating. Women want men who will listen to them and hear their needs and comments.

They want men who are responsive and willing to hear what their partners have to say. And when we say listen we mean really, really listen.

Respectful

This goes without saying. Everyone, both men and women, want to be treated with dignity and respect. They want to be treated right and they deserve that kind of treatment. Always treat your partner like a lady and respect her needs and desires. If you are not willing to do that, you should not be in the relationship in the first place. Poor treatment is a deal breaker for most women. As it should be.

Consistent

While we don't need to be perfect, we need to be consistent. We cannot want one thing today and something totally different the next day and something different on the third day. That drives most people crazy.

People are usually willing to find out what people want and as long as we are consistent our partners will respond accordingly. But when we don't appear to know what we want, how can we expect our partners to know what we want either?

Be consistent and communicate with your partner. Let them know what you want or how you want it. Talk to each other and let each other know the reasons behind the request or actions. By doing this you become closer and form a deeper relationship.

Trustworthy

This is similar to being honest but basically, if you say you are going to do something, do it. If you make a commitment, follow through with it. Always tell the truth and stand behind what you say after you say it.

Women want someone they can rely on and trust. Being able to trust your partner is one of the most important aspects of any kind of relationship.

Romantic

Women love guys to be romantic. They like to be sweet talker and be given flowers for no reason. They love to be swept off their feet and be treated like royalty. When you really get down to it, men love the same things as well.

It is not so much what you do it is that you do something for your partner that is special and romantic.

Keep the spark alive whether you have been together 30 days or 30 years. Romanticism will always be in demand and will never become outdated. So go out and do something that will make her feel loved and appreciated.

Reliable

Everyone likes to have a partner they can count on. They want their partner to be where he said he would be when he said he would be there. They want to believe that when their partner says he will take care of something that it really will be taken care of.

If you say you will pick up the dry cleaning, do your best to pick it up. If you say you will take her to see a show, don't weasel out at the last minute. If she needs you then you should be there. There are a lot of things in life that cannot be depended upon. You should not be one of them!

Show Empathy

Your partner will appreciate your ability to show empathy when things aren't going right. By being there and providing comfort and support even when your partner might be at fault is something that everyone wants from their partners.

Remember that it is sometimes more important to be happy than it is to be right. I'm just sayin'.

Humble

We saved this one for last but it is one of the most important personality traits. While you might be the most interesting or best looking guy on the planet, she doesn't need to be constantly reminded of it. If you are always right, she doesn't need to be reminded of that either!

It is all right to be proud of your skills and accomplishments. But confident people do not feel the need to tell everyone how great they are or all that they have accomplished. They are comfortable with who and what they are without the non-stop bragging.

Believe me when I say that your partner knows about your accomplishments and your abilities and will appreciate your ability to be modest about them. Your partner will appreciate not being reminded about how great you are and how they pale in comparison.

It has been said that a boastful man usually brags to everyone because he has no one to talk to. Don't be a boastful person. Be humble and let your actions speak for themselves. Which they usually will do if you are truly modest.

Sex

Though this is not a book about sex, or how to make sex great, any book about how to be a great boyfriend at least has to cover the basics as far as sex and the relationship are concerned. First and foremost, when it comes to sex, it is critical that you always treat your partner with dignity and respect. That means respecting her wishes and attitudes when it comes to sex.

Sex can be something that brings you and your partner closer together or it can split the two of you apart. Sex drives and desires between two people should be as equal as possible so that neither partner becomes frustrated or angry. This is another one of those areas where communication is the key. Don't just say no or be unresponsive, talk to your partner about why you feel the way you do. Don't ignore problems and think they will go away because they won't.

The sexual response is one that contains both physical and emotional components. It is not possible to separate the two. Sex without emotion is not really sex. It is lust. When you are in a relationship it is an expression of love and attraction between two people that care deeply about each other.

Here are some things you should keep in mind when your relationship reaches the point where sex is introduced or is very close:

Never Violate Trust

When two people have sex, most barriers are down and each partner is at their most vulnerable. Passions and emotions can take things to new levels and both people must remain aware of what they are doing and must never violate the trust that has been created within the relationship.

If you are unsure of whether or not you should do something, then hold off until you either discuss it with your partner or become sure that it's OK. If that means waiting, then wait. If you come on too strong or go to fast, you may scare or frighten your partner and the result is that barriers will be created that may never come back down.

Be Gentle & Loving

Sex should always be gentle and loving. That does not mean that passion cannot kick in and take things to another level. But regardless of where your passions might take you, never inflict pain or discomfort or do anything your partner doesn't like or has not agreed to.

In the beginning, tenderness and affection play an important role in sex. During this time you are in the midst of figuring each other out and determining what each other enjoys and likes. So be gentle and loving and let things take their own course. It is better to take it slow and both be happy than risk going too fast and creating problems.

Respect Her Wishes & Boundaries

There can be many reasons why your partner might not want to do a particular sex act. They may have a moral objection or they might just not enjoy doing something. You need to respect that and not insist or constantly ask for her to do something you know she doesn't enjoy. Remember that sex is supposed to be enjoyable for both people not just one.

If boundaries are set in the relationship and there comes a time you might want to change those boundaries, discuss it in advance. Do not surprise your partner by trying something you previously agreed was off limits.

Talk to her first and talk things through. If she agrees then try it and see how it goes. If she refuses, do not try it anyway. Respect her wishes.

That being said, it is important that your sex life is fulfilling for both of you. If your sex drive or desires are too different there might not be any way to compromise and at that point the relationship might have to end so that both of you can find a suitable partner. Or, both of you might decide that sex is not that important and that other areas of your relationship are so great the sex doesn't matter.

But if that is the case, both people have to be completely honest. The human sex drive is very strong and if some person wants sex more often than the other, or if they want something the other person is not willing to provide, that can cause significant problems for both of you.

Take it Slow

When you first introduce sex into the relationship, take it slow. Take your time, concentrate on foreplay, and make sure she gets as much out of the experience as possible. Don't worry about your performance

. Pressure will only make things worse. For both of you the focus should be on being closer than ever before and enjoying something new and special between you.

Do not be in a hurry to introduce new things and swing from the chandeliers or anything like that. There is a lot of time for experimentation and growth. Don't rush things. Quality is much more important than quantity.

Moving ahead at a slow pace also helps you partner to relax and become more at ease and confident in their sexual performance. Expecting too much too soon might introduce so much pressure that the act itself will lose much of its wonder and appeal.

Know What She Wants

When it comes to sex, try and be aware of what she wants out of the experience. Try and determine what she likes and what she dislikes. Listen for her breathing and reactions to things that you do. Discover her sensitive spots and learn what kind of touch she likes.

This is all part of getting to know each other and it can be one of the most enjoyable and important parts of the relationship. Both of you are opening yourself up to each other and telling yourself that it is all right to allow yourself to be vulnerable.

Don't just be concerned with your needs or how it feels to you. Concentrate on her and her experience. There are a lot of guys who are interested in just what they want and what feels good for them. Don't be that guy. Be the guy who your partner appreciates for thinking of her needs as well as your own.

Sometimes Just Hug Her

We already mentioned this but it bears repeating. It is all right to just hug and kiss and cuddle. It doesn't always have to lead to sex or passion. Sometimes just the closeness and intimacy is enough for both of you.

The problem arises when it is enough for one but the other wants to go further. When that happens, communication is the key to avoiding hurt feelings and frustration. Try and discuss things and work out a resolution that is acceptable to both of you.

But whatever you do, never force anyone to do anything they are not comfortable with and never violate the trust that has been built in the relationship. There is not an orgasm in the world that is worth risking that!

Protection

Keep in mind that there are health reasons and other reasons for having protected sex especially for the first time. Each partner should assume responsibility for birth control and protection from disease. Though it might be a delicate conversation, you should make sure each partner is free of sexually transmitted diseases.

Even if your partner says they have no diseases it is still a good idea to use a condom in case they were less than truthful. Your life is important and you should do whatever you can to protect both you and your partner from any disease or unwanted pregnancy.

Sex is an important part of every relationship. But sex will be better if you wait until both of you are ready for it. Do not rush into it and make sure you are prepared both physically and emotionally for the experience. Pick the right place, the right time and the right circumstances for your first time. You can only have your first time once and you should do your best to make it special and memorable.

This is not mean to be a complete guide or resource on the sexual aspect of your relationship. There are entire books written on this subject and we suggest you read a dedicated book on the subject if you feel the need to do so. Our intent at this point is just to give you a few things to think about when it comes to introducing sex into your relationship.

Although each of us are different in our own ways, if we truly care about our partners and wish to do what makes them happy, our hearts will usually be taken in the right direction. Be aware of what is going on and your partner's reactions to certain things. Keep in mind that her views towards sex are likely to follow the same course as other parts of her life.

If she is shy and reserved she is likely to be the same way when it comes to sex. This is not right or wrong. It is just how she is and you need to respect that. You need to proceed in the direction your partner leads you and at a pace that both of you feel comfortable. Never force, never rush, and never make your partner fell guilty or inadequate. If you adhere to all the above then your relationship will have an even better chance of growing and getting stronger over time.

Be Spontaneous

Show me someone who is predictable and I will show you someone who is boring. Boring people might be very well intentioned and they might mean very well in the process but they are still boring. Most people crave some form of excitement or surprises in their lives. They want to wonder what will happen next. They don't want their entire life scripted and predictable.

Sometimes the little surprises in life make the most impact. The boyfriend who constantly thinks of ways to make life interesting and spontaneous is a great boyfriend. We already mentioned a few things you can do to shake things up and add a little suspense and thrills to your relationship. We highly advise you to do some of those things and do them regularly.

The key is to every so often do the unexpected. Keep her a little off balances and thinking about what is going to happen next. Never let her get bored with you. A great boyfriend keeps the passions and interest at a high level at all times!

Keep the Relationship Fresh

Sometimes after two people have known each other for some time they get too comfortable with each other. They go to the same restaurants, watch the same TV shows and do the same things every night. They know what each other wants or likes and that's what they do. It is all very nice but not very good.

When this happens, search for somewhere new to go or something new to do. Sign up for a class on something the two of you are interested in such as painting or dancing. Get out with different people and do different things.

Give Her a Present When She Doesn't Expect One!

Anyone can come up with a present on a birthday or holiday. Show up every now and then with a small present or some flowers. Send flowers to her work.

She might love that her co-workers see that she has such a thoughtful and caring boyfriend. It never hurts to have people compliment her about you!

The presents don't have to cost a lot of money. In these cases the thought really does matter the most! Sometimes a little gift can go a long way.

Make Her Laugh

Everyone likes to laugh. Be the person who makes her laugh. Don't take yourself and life too seriously. A career and earning money is one thing but the ability to make other people laugh is a great ability to have.

Just be careful not to make her laugh at someone else's expense and be aware of her sense of humor beforehand. Some of us find different things funny so make sure you know what she finds amusing.

The time you spend together should be positive and upbeat. A great boyfriend will concentrate on having fun and creating happy and funny memories. If you can do that, your relationship will become stronger and closer. After all, we all need a little bit of time where we can let our hair down, relax, and have a good laugh!

Don't be Passive

Sometimes we are so focused on doing what she likes we allow her to make all the decisions. We go along with everything she asks, everything she suggests, and the relationship becomes one sided. While some women might like this, the vast majority would like to see the man take the lead some of the time.

That means taking an active role in what you do and how your relationship progresses. It means asserting yourself from time to time to make sure you do some of the things that you like to do. Suggest the place you go for dinner, buy tickets to a show you think you will both like. Just take an active role once in a while.

This helps both people get more of what they want in the relationship while at the same time removing all the pressure off of the one person who usually determines what you are going to do. Women like a take charge type of person who is not overpowering at the same time. As with most parts of a relationship, balance in the key.

Never Be Boring

No one likes a boring person. Boring is predictable and boring is, well, just boring. You should be the person who brings excitement and fun into the relationship.

If you are the person who comes over and does the same things, day in and day out, that's just boring.

Vary the conversation. Don't talk about problems at work all the time or about the same things all the time. Learn about new things to talk about. Draw her into conversations and listen to what is going on in her life. The conversations should be varied and not just about you. Her life and experiences and problems are just as important to her as yours are to you. Be the person who listens to her and keeps things upbeat and happy.

Take a Trip

Nothing says romance and fun than a trip to somewhere new. Not only do you get to experience something new, but taking a trip together also means plenty of private and alone time as well. Surprise her with a short trip to an interesting place and she will appreciate the gesture.

This doesn't have to be an exotic or expensive place but it shouldn't be boring either. Pick a place that has some unique places to see and things to do. Plan the whole trip and take care of all the arrangements. Take control of the whole trip and make it special for the two of you.

One thing to consider is the stage of the relationship. In the very beginning going away together might be too frightening for both of you. There would be the pressure of spending so much time together and even sharing a room or bed. If that is an issue then book two rooms to take that pressure away. Always remember the focus of the trip should be to relax and enjoy each other not make each other tense and scared.

When it comes to being spontaneous, that means doing the unexpected and being able to do things on the spur of the moment. It means being able to do things at the last minute without a ton of planning and forethought. An example might be just deciding to go to a museum or park you have never been to before and doing that right now when the idea hits you.

Being spontaneous lends a little spice to the day and helps keep things fresh and alive. Everyone likes a little excitement and variation in their lives. Be that person for your girlfriend. You will both appreciate it. And you will have a lot of laughs in the process!

Be Independent

While our girlfriends like us to focus on them and their needs, they also like to have their own time and not feel smothered by the men in their lives. This is not a sexist comment because men feel the same way. In fact, no one likes to feel that someone else always there and always wants something from us or make demands on us.

Everyone needs to run their own lives and have the time to do the things that they want to do or even do nothing at all. As partners we need to understand that and not be angry or sad when our partner tells us that just is going out with friends or just wants to spend time alone tonight with a good book.

Time apart is good for every relationship because it reinforces what it is that we love about our partner. We miss the laughter, the physical connection and the company our partners provide to us.

When that is missing for a while, we appreciate it even more. That helps us stay focused on why our partners are so special to us.

Spending every minute of every day together can place a strain on any relationship. That is why relationships between people who work together sometimes are so difficult to maintain. You wake up together, go to work together, come home together and spend every minute together. Sometimes too much of a good thing is not a good thing after all!

So now that we agree that a little "alone time" is a good thing, here are a few other things to consider as you try to become a little bit more independent:

Don't Be Jealous

Jealous people are a real downer for most women. Jealousy tells her that you don't trust her. It also tells her that you are very insecure in the relationship and probably insecure in yourself as well. Neither of those is very appealing or viewed as positives by your partner.

Instead, let her know you trust her. Don't ask her questions about where she went, who she went with, what time she got home or anything else along those lines.

Trust her to be straight with you and always be truthful. Unless she gives you a valid reason to feel otherwise, give her the space and trust she needs and deserves.

Take Care of Yourself

You are not her responsibility when it comes to taking care of yourself. That is on you and no one else. Your partner should be part of your happiness not responsible for it. Get a hobby or other outside interests to spend your time when you are not together. Take a class, go to a movie, go out with friends and do other things to give you a satisfactory social life when she is not around.

Take care of your physical appearance and your emotional state as well. Do not be sad or depressed when your partner is not with you. You have a life outside the relationship and you need to take care of that as well.

Spend Time with Your Friends

Chances are you had friends before you met your partner and you should not neglect or ignore them now. Clear time in your schedule to keep in touch and spend time with your friends. This is an important part of your social life.

Always remember that sometimes relationships do come to an end. If this happens to you and you have neglected or ignored your friends you might find yourself without a support structure or much of a social life. Balance is the key. Make time for your friends and your partner. Integrate your relationship into your circle of friends if that is possible as well.

Give Her Space

Don't keep her from her friends and family. Make plans for alone time and time with friends. Don't pressure her to spend every night and day with you. Have a friend's night out once a week or whenever both of you feel it should be.

Talk to each other and make sure each of you has the time they need outside the relationship to pay attention to the other parts of their lives. Doing so now will enable you to build a solid relationship that doesn't replace your previous lives but instead becomes an important part of your life. In order to be in a relationship with you should not mean she has to give up everything else. If you demand this from her, she will soon resent you for it.

Don't Be Clingy or Needy

Women like to feel that they are an important part of your life but they do NOT want someone who is clingy, whiney or needy. This indicates weakness on the part of the man and that is not a good way for your partner to see you.

Instead, let her know that you need her but also show her that you are fully able to function without her constantly near you to help you. Be able to accept time apart and don't sit home and brood. Cultivate other parts of your life when she isn't there.

This will not make her feel that she isn't important so don't worry about that. Instead, it shows her that you have the strength to live your life and that can take a lot of pressure off her. She will not resent you for this. In fact, chances are she will respect you and feel more positively towards you and having you in her life.

Don't Be Controlling

If you want to make a relationship end really, really fast, be a controlling person. Tell her what she needs to do and make sure she does just that and nothing else. She will soon be heading for the hills or to the local courts for a restraining order!

Relationships need to be give and take and not controlled by just one person.

You should never keep her from doing the things she likes or seeing the people she wants to see. Do not isolate her from her family or friends. Do not tell her what to do, how to dress or what to say. That will be the quickest way to destroy the relationship.

Controlling people are often extremely insecure and are worried that they will lose their partner if she is able to see other people or talk to other people. They are afraid that they will find themselves alone and will do anything to make that doesn't happen.

Controlling behavior is abusive behavior. You need to be open and honest and talk through things. No one should be controlled or prohibited from living their lives as they see fit. If you ever find yourself in that sort of relationship, it probably is time to leave and find someone else.

Maintain Individual Interests

Sure it is nice to have the same interests but we are still individuals and we cannot expect to be so compatible that we don't have interests and hobbies they other might not like or enjoy. Just because we are in relationships does not mean we have to sacrifice the rest of our identity.

While we should at least make an effort to share our interests and passions, if our partner does not wish to share them with us, we should continue to keep them as part of our life. That gives us something to do when we are not with our partners and allows us to continue to enjoy the thing in our lives that we take pleasure in.

Your partner should not discourage you from continuing these activities unless they interfere with your relationship or your ability to spend time together. The same goes for you as well. You should never try and stop your partner from doing things she finds enjoyable or rewarding as well. Keep your common interests and supplement them with individual interests to make the entire relationship happy and rewarding.

Trust Her

One of the key parts of any relationship, whether it is a romantic or platonic relationship, is that both people trust each other. That means both partners are honest and truthful with one another and they have complete faith and confidence that their partners are behaving and acting appropriately when they are apart.

That means no questioning your partner about where they were or what they did.

It means trusting them enough to not be jealous or angry when they tell you they are spending time with friends. It also means not playing games with them or making them feel guilty for doing things or going places without you.

Remember, when you enter a relationship both people do not give up who they are or what their lives were before you. Instead, both of your need to combine your lives to create a new life for the both of you. It is then both of your responsibility to blend both old and new lives together.

Better Yourself

Sometimes the best thing you can do for your partner is to take care of yourself. After all, you are a reflection on your partner. When others look at you, they will see her as well. You want to make sure you cast a positive shadow over her in the eyes of others.

As far as your partner is concerned, when she looks at you, she must see something positive in your to remain in the relationship. That doesn't mean you have to be perfect or look like a model or anything like that. But you have to inspire confidence and a positive feeling in the eyes of your partner in order for the relationship to grow and flourish.

Another reason for you to take care of yourself and your life is because it shows that you care about your life and your role in it.

It shows responsibility and self confidence. It tells other that you have your act together and that you have a bright future ahead of you. It also tells your partner that building a future with you will be promising.

Like it or not, relationships are built on trust and security, If you take care of yourself and inspire confidence in the eyes of your partner the relationship will grow. If she looks at you and sees someone who is messy, poorly groomed and content to sit on the couch and play video games 20 hours a day that is not likely going to create a positive feeling in her mind.

But you should be doing this for yourself and not because of what someone else wants to see in you. You should be doing this because you take pride in not only who you are but what you have accomplished in your life. Women like confident men and they like to see some level of ambition in their men at the same time.

So now that we know why we should be taking care of ourselves, here are a few things we should be aware of to help us get started:

Take Care of Your Body

Like we said already, taking care of your body does not mean you have to look like a cover model.

You don't need to spend hours at the gym every day or be buffed or ripped either. But you should keep yourself in reasonably good condition.

That means keeping your weight under control and watching what you eat and your overall health. We only get one chance in life and we want our lives to be as long and healthy as possible. Eat healthy, exercise and get regular check-ups and medical evaluations. As you get older you should see doctors and specialists more often.

Think of this as helping you and your partner spend many more years together. You also want your partner to look at you and feel attraction not repulsion. Do it for yourself and your partner. Because your health is something that is of prime importance to both of you.

Have Goals in Your Life

Women look for men in their lives who have goals and dreams. They want men who are not satisfied with what they have today but are always looking for bigger and better things in life. This does not mean they are superficial or overly concentrate on material things. It does mean that they are looking for men who have goals and dreams that they want to pursue.

You can tell a lot from what a man wants out of life. If they have their eyes set on a better job, or if they are working towards an important goal in their lives, that shows a lot about the man's character. Women look for men who have dreams and expectations. They usually do not want someone who lives for today and doesn't plan for the future.

But like with most things in life women also want someone who takes the time to enjoy life in the moment as well. So balance is the key when it comes to enjoying now and preparing for then. Take the time to spend time with each other and enjoy the joys and excitement of what is going on now. But at the same time, plan out where you want to go in life and what it is going to take to get your there.

The earlier in your life that you start preparing for your future the easier it is going to be. But don't spend so much time planning for the future that you totally miss out on what is going on now. The things you do today will become your memories of tomorrow.

Have Values & Morals in Your Life

Though this might never come up in normal conversation, women like men with high values and morals.

They want someone who is going to stand behind what they say and do and that have a moral code that helps guide them throughout their lives. Security is something that is very important in life and if you are a person with high moral character that will inspire confidence and peace of mind in your partner as well.

Women also like successful men but only those who go about it in the right way. They want people who go about things honestly and are not willing to lie, cheat and steal just to get what they want in life. Money is not everything and personal integrity is something that most women admire greatly in the men.

They realize that their man is a reflection of them and they want their men to be well respected and admired. Since that is the case, they will almost always pick someone with at least as high a moral character as they have. So do both you and your partner a favor and establish a good set of morals and values. Once you have established them, stick with them every day.

Improve Your Knowledge & Skills

One of the best ways to improve yourself is to become more knowledgeable. Read books, watch the news, study things that are important in the world and learn more about the things that are important to your partner as well.

Increasing your knowledge makes you more valuable to society and worth more in the marketplace as well. Knowledge is power and it is also useful to be able to talk intelligently at parties and social gatherings. The more you know, the more impressive you can be in the eyes of others. Don't be a know it all and don't be pompous but strive to learn more whenever you get the chance.

Take a few classes to earn your degree or prepare yourself for a new and better job. Whatever it might be that you want to do, take the bull by the horns and make it happen. Share with her what you are doing and why you are doing it. Make her part of it especially if it could impact the time the two of you can spend together.

Learn Something New that She Likes

It is always good to try something new in life. Since you are open to this anyway, why not see if something she enjoys might also interest you as well? This will not only give you more time together but it will also give you something else in common between the two of you.

If she enjoys shows, try and learn about some of the most popular shows. Grab a few tickets and go to them with her. Make an effort to see if some of the things she likes are interesting to you as well.

Just making the effort to try and enjoy some of her favorite things will be greatly appreciated by your partner.

This does not mean you have to continue if you find it really hard to enjoy something she really likes. If that is the case, give it a try and if it doesn't work out, let her know that. Remember honesty is important. Your partner will not want you to do something you really hate.

But, and this is a big but, as part of a relationship you should be agreeable to do some things you partner like and enjoys just because you want to make her happy. You might not enjoy a Broadway show but go to one once in a while. Even buy the tickets and surprise her. She will appreciate your sacrifice and it will make her feel good. You don't get to avoid everything you don't enjoy and she doesn't either!

Make Her a Part of Your Improvement

If your relationship has progressed to this point, consider making your partner part of your improvement process. Ask her what things she thinks you might improve upon. But be prepared for the answers! You might be told something you really didn't want to hear! But if the suggestions make sense to you, why not tackle things one by one until you have hit most or all of them?

One more thing about improvement.

Life and improvement go hand in hand. We never really stop learning and improving. We should be constantly learning, adapting and living life to the fullest. It can be very tempting to sit back and rest and enjoy things are they currently are. But if we do this for too long a period of time, something else happens.

When we fail to improve while those around us do improve, we find ourselves suddenly moving backwards. When we stay the same while others get better, they move ahead of us and we fall behind. So don't let that happen to you. Keep improving and keep pushing yourself forward.

As far as your relationships are concerned, always remember that relationships are living, breathing and changing things. As we change our relationships change as well. Hopefully those changes are for the best but sometimes they might be for the worst. Keeping your eyes and ears open and changing gradually to adapt to change is one of the best ways to keep your relationship open, honest, and changing.

Conclusion

First of all, give yourself a pat on the back for reading through this entire book. Just the act of taking the time to read this book sets you ahead of most people when it comes to really wanting to be a great boyfriend and partner. While some are content to do whatever they feel they should, you have taken it one step further. You deserve a pat on the back for that my friend!

As you read through this book you probably found a lot of things you agreed with and a few that you never even thought about before. At least I hope that was the case. While a lot of the material in this book might appear to be common sense, you would be surprised at how many people never even think about those things.

It is not because these are bad or evil people. It might just be that they weren't awarded. The great news is that you are now aware of those things.

The bad news is that you are now aware of those same things so you have no excuse!

Hopefully you are already doing most of the things suggested in this book. That is usually the case. In that case all you will need to do is make some minor modifications in the way you approach your relationships and treat your partners. For most of us that is a relatively minor and easy process. Just take your time and use some common sense and you should do just fine.

If you found a lot of things that you think you need to work on, relax a bit because that isn't so hard either especially if you move ahead the right way. The key to making a lasting and effective change is to change one or two things at a time until they become part of you and require no thought or effort. Sort of like practice makes perfect.

Pick one or two things that you feel are the most important and that will give you the greatest impact and get started with those things. First, figure out how to best implement those things into your life. Sometimes the best success comes when you carefully plan out how to do something the right way.

Then move forward and change one or two behaviors. Do not push too hard or expect too much of yourself. Don't try to do too much too soon. Speed is not the most important thing. Success is more important than speed. Take things slow and then get down to it.

Check from time to time to see how you are doing. Sometimes we have to make little tweaks or changes to our approach to become more successful. There is nothing wrong with that approach. Everything should be focused on getting the best results. We can make mistakes in the process. That's OK as most of us will make mistakes. But if we learn from those mistakes we will just become stronger and more effective in the future!

Always remember that what you change today will keep giving you benefits for years to come. It is worth giving your best effort. Not only will your life better but your partner's life will be better as well. Your relationships will be stronger, your emotional connections will be deeper and everything will be more fulfilling and rewarding.

So let's get moving!

Made in the USA
Monee, IL
09 February 2023

27385361R00072